Elixir

Books by Janine Certo

In the Corner of the Living

Children Writing Poems: Poetic Voices In and Out of School

Elixir

Poems by Janine Certo

NEW AMERICAN PRESS + BORDIGHERA PRESS

Co-published by

NEW AMERICAN PRESS
P. O. Box 1094
Grafton, WI 53024

BORDIGHERA PRESS
John D. Calandra Italian American Institute
25 W. 43rd Street, 17th Floor
New York, NY 10036

Cover features *Bottle* by Gertrude Lemberg, Courtesy National Gallery of Art, Washington.

Library of Congress Control Number: 2021935085

New American Poetry Prize 2020
Lauria/Frasca Poetry Prize 3
ISBN 978-1-941561-24-9

TABLE OF CONTENTS

For my mother and brother, and for Steve
In memory of my father

Elixir: A sovereign remedy for illness; a strong extract or tincture; the quintessence or soul of a thing; its home kernel or secret principle.

OXFORD ENGLISH DICTIONARY

With what joy I am carrying
a case of wine up a mountain—

W.S. MERWIN

Everything takes form, even infinity.

GASTON BACHELARD, *THE POETICS OF SPACE*

Drag Heavy Pot to Shed (Ars Poetica I)

Squint at the barred owl, then race down
the steep hill of your childhood. You lost
the dog but found your grandmother
who drank a bottle of rubbing alcohol. Shake
her ten times. Prepare a fine cheese, sliced peach,
hazelnuts. Drizzle with honey. Slide it under
the bed to the monster. Hear the crack in a mother's
voice who says it would be so easy to go down to
the garage, turn the ignition on. What will you do with all this
moonlight on the pond, at once galaxy, scattered
photons, shards of glass? If you want truth, see
how the Pope's Swiss Guard curses at tourists,
throws stones at pigeons in the square. Play a game
of Chase the Trees for leaves like wine in a human
heart—darker than the blood it pumps, the beating
silence in those hours cleaning after they took away
your father's body. I tell you, we cannot say love
enough times. The vacuum's defective, so it sings.
Write until the sage & fir candle kills the smell
of the wall's rotting mouse. Look over your
shoulder for the child you never had, the sibling
you left in the front yard, the dog returning, bread
in her mouth. Revisit title. Now your words are the
loose parts of a rocking chair, the longing for meadow—
some ground of consciousness, what the philosopher
called the dialectic of inside-outside. And when you're
close, smear the shapes of ghosts. Draw grief a warm bath.
Lately, there is little spring or fall, but keep the large bright
mum in its pot until the flowers are dull, their necks broken.

INTIMATE IMMENSITY

After Rescuing the Dying Butterfly from My Sidewalk

The woman at the Wildlife
Rehabilitation Center
put me on hold,

came back to say
don't bother. It would be dead
in two to six weeks.

I picked it out of the shoebox:
head, thorax & abdomen
tilted over, a sailboat

with a torn jib. I gently
pinched its wings, trimmed
the black margins

until both wings
were even-sized. I clipped
paper the size of the damaged

spot, dabbed glue on the repair site,
& considered my foolish
stubbornness as I applied

powder, its legs still kicking.
In the garden beds,
my monarch slipped

down a stick, labored
to open its new wings,
& just when I thought

the effort failed, it flew away.
How short of a life would it take
to matter? How many

of us travel roads
before rigs shift gears
surrounding us like barricades

with their diesel & cargo;
or keep away from water for the scratch
of blood coral, the brush of a ray?

We board up windows to stave
off hurricanes that tumble
at us like hay bales

or avoid the atmosphere
unexplored, never booking
the morning's first flight.

I want to know the symmetry
of a monarch,
how it enjoys this sweet

bright life full of heartbeat
& memory, as if
there would always

be milkweed & an infinite
variety of flowers.

Agoraphobia

On my knees before the first leaves to open—
JENNIFER MILITELLO

You're reminded of walking
paths picking strawberries,

dogwoods scattering their white,
how all that outside waits,

some winged thing between
window & screen & for no

reason, ground swell: extraction
of air, a geodesy flipped like

hands slipping off the Earth
or missing the exit & caught

in a line of cars, semis, a hundred
moths colliding, rising in your chest

& the heart's misfiring, then
over a bridge then catapulting

through a tunnel, the darkness
an interminable river & someone

keeps mouthing *Bend backwards*
over this mountain.

Holding Hands on the Bank. Leaves Float down the River.

that spring   your father sick suddenly—
                                         a degenerative brain disease
a one in one million chance   & while you were out of town
                                         caring for him
like a record skipping   you had to keep telling him

it was no one's fault
our dog seized repeatedly   he would die

                                         next spring
as peony petals dropped   at a tray table
                                         we took turns
                                         in a faded green chair
                                         with my own father in hospice

we said goodbye to friends:
one a heart attack
the other pancreatic cancer—
one who wrote   asking: *When are you coming here*
                                         again?

the other phoning
from a canyon:
God, I wish you could see this
his motorcycle gleaming   at the edge

                                         he was so thin you said
                                         you could see through him

you went into the forest
then I went in

                    we learned
                    how to talk someone
                    to the other side

Love,
I'll always look for you
on the other side   so long as there is one

Landscape with River, Man, Mountain

> There are not enough seats
> in the steel lifeboat for everybody.
> U.S. STEEL EXECUTIVE, 1975

Before the layoffs, we children watched
men hefting coal, huddling at the shore,
their lunch boxes flashing with flicks
from an oiled sun and their thermoses
like rescue flares. Facing the Works,

we ate pizza and dust, vines of crown
vetch all around—one spill of red
blossom in our landscape. The smell
of sulfur still moves me. A blast I never
saw, colorless in the air, but I knew

something was lost, like benzene
or fleeting particulates: a train pushing
Rt. 1 on the bank; a barge steaming
from Pittsburgh; an oak disappearing
in the waters, and an unemployed

father who shot himself, his ghost
mowing the lawn, nodding as we
walked past. The odor of my town
was dough, stale egg, cut grass. I couldn't
wait to get out. I can never go back.

Childhood Friends

Our childhoods still hum in the static
of a transistor radio & the watery
memory of my parents' above-ground pool,
each of us on different rafts, drawing the handles
tight to make one float, the long length

of our legs touching, our form spinning
in & out of shade, lifting our bikinis to view
our tan lines, our mothers weeding the hill—
bent like pitched tents. The bells of St. Michael's
Church & the ice cream truck caroled as we drifted—

a small continent under an atmosphere busy
with clouds, wondering where all
the planes were going, never getting the words
right to Pink Floyd's *Another Brick in the Wall*.
Remember when we planned to live together?

We'd be Laverne & Shirley skipping
an American street, arm in arm, reciting
a Yiddish hopscotch chant. *Let's get together
next year*, is a grief that pools in my chest,
a steady low frequency, like the low notes

of a ballad, because I'm still not sure
how it happens, who gets tired or who changes
directions first, but I remember
the release, seeing you float to the other side,
each of us reaching one arm under the sun

as if all we believed was at stake, one arm
outstretched as a last impossible chance
before we sang goodbye.

Highland Meadows, Allegheny County, 1979

Sunday afternoons, we escaped across green waves
of fenceless yards, hopscotched streets with split-
level homes—their windowed eyes and garages' open
mouths. We screamed past the chained

    dog's bark, lawns skirted with azaleas
    or crowned with the Virgin Mary.
    We lifted animals like bracelets from creeks
    and sat on Central Pharmacy's curb snapping twigs
    of Kit Kat, hot gravel beneath our soles.

    At the playground, we bounced
    on air, child gods attempting
    to hook our feet. From there, dogwoods
    were bouquets, and hemlocks raised us
    on the tips of their fingers.

        Five o' clock screen doors diffused marinara,
        stuffed cabbage, or *pasta fazool*—thick as glory.

        Evenings, we circled a bottle, tongued
        cones twisted like snow-wrapped
        mountains, biked down vertical
        roads, the rush of our tires muffling

the coal train. Nighttime, we marked our bodies
on driveways like Xs as if the stars said we were done.

    Fathers' voices rocked back porches, while
    mothers chatted above the crickets, their gossip
    a red lip. As we slept in our beds,

adults watched lives played back at them: their own, or maybe
a life they tried to show up for or tried to make, but
eventually let go, like a morning bus any child could miss.

One Life Burning

Cone Snail Venom Relieves Pain
Finds Filipino Scientist
THE PITTSBURGH POST-GAZETTE

I'm reading for my father: ill
going on thirty years. He told me
neuropathy was like a hundred
needles coursing the whole body.

What is it like to live your one life
burning? Maybe it is easier to kill
than to keep the living alive,
but I remember my father before

his eyes turned over to stones
smoothed with fear's glaze. Hope
is yet another drug, *Prialt*,
which claims to lessen the barbed

missiles of pain. I think of this one
doctor in his lab, Olivera,
the only doctor who
gently milks the snails, entices

each one to pierce a covered
test tube opening, despite
another Philippine typhoon,
wall of ocean surging, loved ones

swept away, homes destroyed.
I've watched a cone snail close up
harpoon a common beach worm,
the worm retracting swiftly into a coil,

paralyzed on the shore. My father
taught me as a child to toss back empty
shells to the sea, to bury snails
in the sand, everything except its head

so it could breathe. This is a poem
for that one doctor who works to relieve pain,
for my mother who always picks up
shells on the beach, for my father who,

when I read him the headline, asked,
What happens to the cone snails?

Halftime

A San Giorgio box squat by the stove,
sautéed garlic, onion, tomato paste,
salted water, where meaning
took shape in olive oil, wine, oregano, basil,
a wood spoon bleeding on the counter,
mist from the colander
transforming kitchen to steam room,
an omnipotent god exhaling warm
wind, my mother preparing salad, yelling
for my brother & me to come, the dog
at our feet as we fed from the endless
platter, pulling from a loaf of Italian,
hooking tubes with our forks, the game
almost back on, dipping our bread
in the dressing at the bottom of the bowl,
never imagining this could all be gone.

HOUSE AND UNIVERSE

Sibling with Hair on Fire. Sibling Tangled in Vines.

I don't know why I keep bringing up
    the time I emerged from the thicket
with a bucket of berries, and you
    seized it from me and ran …

but even now, brother, on the phone,
    you are so far away. When we visit,
it's hurricane and lightning
    and the cell you keep checking,

while I want to make sense
    of being pulled from where the salt-
loving algae makes the rivers
    run red. What I mean is this:

I'm still lost in the thorny bramble,
    looking for your outstretched hand.
I'm sorry for assuming you didn't know
    what *autobiography* meant. You're sorry

for mocking me for ordering the impossible
    burger. For too long, we kept trying to find
glint in a cereal spoon, the pilfered spirit,
    the ball thrown in the house,

the lighted tree down, the porcelain
    figurine, its head severed. Does it matter
who took branches, muck, leaves
    from the teeth of a gaping fender,

or who refused to dissect a pig, but touched
      the inside of its small, pale heart?
Acceptance is
      our dying father attempting

to stand, falling into us, how so many
      poems begin with *After*. Brother, we
would have met in any other place like this:
      the sun with its relentless fire,
      the steeple shooting the sky with blue.

When They Named the Egret and Kept Feeding Her

As a child, I sat on the cold edge
of the bathtub & watched her
seal a lip with a Kleenex, swipe
mascara with a wand. She saw me
in the mirror, her wide-set eyes

tucked under a blow-out
like Jackie O. I asked: *Aren't you
ever afraid of getting it in your eye?*
In the Middle Ages, women burned
cork to lengthen lashes, used

brushes made of feather
& bone. Lead paint poisoned
hundreds for a Mask of Youth
like Queen Elizabeth I, then came
Coco-Chanel, L'Oréal, more

animal & mineral to name
women: *Object of Gaze.* Which is
all to say my own face drops
when my mother, who has learned
how to feed every kind of bird

from her hands, who saved two
human lives by giving CPR, who runs
out for a card when anyone dies, who
when I snap the photo,
think she looks the same—

she is the beginning, middle & end
of everything, I have to tell you, I'm
on the edge of the Gulf & I show her
her photo on my phone & she begs me:
Get rid of it. I hit delete, considering

this construction, beauty. Mother,
it is history & you still standing at the edge
of the water like you stood at the edge
of the sink, just about to begin, face
naked as you flash that open-mouth smile.

Dear Australia,

I'm on a Florida beach, a plane piping plume like at the end
of a politician's cigar. Yesterday, the paper ran a story about
iguanas being sold for their flesh. Cold temperatures paralyze
them until they fall from the canopy like large branches. I
found myself looking for one, needing to pick it up, carry its
tuberculate heft into the brush, risk the bite, the loss of bird
eggs, the locals' hibiscus, because who could heal from your
headlines of cubs bruised like fruit, koalas stunned on earth,
giving up looking for their young? A girl on the beach is now
building a wall of stones to protect her sandcastle that later
will be demolished. *God of orange sky, smoke like coiled rope,*
isn't each animal grievable? I can't unsee the photo of a kangaroo
who couldn't free herself from barbed wire, a snake jumping
the flames, or the wallaby licking our faults from his paws.
It's starting to rain. From oceans away, my prayers are bees.
I gather stones charred to coal. I'm scrounging for any living
stems of Cooktown Orchid, Bottle Brush, Desert Rose. I'm
potting them around a mass grave.

Losing a Religion

> Beyond the window, some kind of small,
> black thing shot across the sky.
>
> HARUKI MURAKAMI

Once on a run, wildflowers by the road, but
      when I called into the canyon, nothing
came back. Once, I restored a ceiling, but
      water kept seeping: saltpeter, soot
and dirt. Too much efflorescence. I tried to rub
      a fresco with bread, dipped a sponge
into wine. A statue looked sullen, split at the eye.

Each time someone loses a religion, a rock
      gets kicked up by a semi, leaving
a fissure on a windshield the shape of a web
      like the one a spider clutches in my house
where I turn pages of poems: the landscapes
      so dark, a patch of river drenched in light.
I picked morels from a church courtyard, folded

      an omelet the color of transcendence.
If I could, I would smooth all the stones. I would
      gather the world's suffering and arrange
it into lilies, even as ants scatter over their petals.
      I believe in new edges: the trees rustling
like breath, the grace of soft rain, knowing
      the long blade will keep coming
back, but when I open my palm, it bursts
            a thousand small birds.

The Childfree Couple

They're on their fourth dog,
a little late

to family gatherings where
relatives have stopped asking.

They've got a guest room
painted crisp white, a ceramic

pitcher of lavender, books
on the nightstand: *Soul*

Without Shame, Creative Cooking
For Two, How to Travel.

Kids sometimes stop by their
house with its different rules:

the chocolate drawer, music
in the back room, a piece of fish

with its head on and a strange
leaf served at bedtime

hours. They drink cocktails
in a garden with no plastic

swimming pools, no swing sets.
They read on an unstained couch

in the shape of an L.
Not a shriek. Not a crash.

Not a sound. *Isn't this nice?*
They tell themselves

there's more time
for each other, art-making, aging

parents, that there's overpopulation,
sex with the door open, the night

a calm ocean. Twice they saw
a child that would have looked like their

own. An ad with a girl under a tree,
tendrils at her face, a branch

in her mouth, and twins
at a gelato stand, the boy tugging

one parent as the other paid,
the girl turning to catch this couple

staring, the one who gave a half smile,
then turned away.

Diamond Doves

I woke to empty cages.
Even at eight, I knew

my grandmother's doves
shouldn't be released.

They have poor homing
instincts. She claimed

their cooing was too much.
That's when I first saw her

illness, cut in the open
and loosed, volatile

as any cat or hawk.
I still remember how

they loved to be stroked
and held. They used to sit

on our fingers, their four eyes
lucid and bright as gemstones.

My Father Asks What I Think Happens after We Die

Remember that picture I took of you waiting
outside Palais Royal? You were banked by rows
of shade trees, each one beautiful as a dead relative.
Wasn't that a time when everything was just
so, when after, we all had that picnic on the grass
with wine, cheese and chocolates resembling stars?

Ode to Pizza

At the first stop in Brooklyn, served from a window,
        I imagined Travolta in *Saturday Night Fever*,
red-collared, a bird of paradise strutting with a double
        folded over, reminding me the best

I ever had was after sex with Jimmy Zito, cold
        as November morning. In Bensonhurst,
one was fermented with a starter. In the oven,
        a *capricciosa* billowed. In Queens, women circled

a pepperoni like at a teen's birthday, friends rehearsing
        their kindnesses. Manhattan evoked the ones
I ordered late, my mind drifting in the spotlight
        of the TV. In the Bronx, it was clam pie

with construction workers & a homeless man shuffling
        back to his shopping cart. We all balanced
our paper plate boats under a noon-blistered sun.
        In Staten Island, I learned about the Neopolitan:

rest dough for six hours; knead by hand; stretch to no more
        than thirty-five centimeters in diameter, rising
to two at the edge. Prepare with basil, tomato, cheese
        from the southern Apennine mountains

or buffalo mozzarella from regione della Campagnia.
        The smell is primal, connecting to lineages
who ate flatbread, Neolithic tribes who cooked batter
        on stones. As the bus droned back over

the Verrazzano, I thought of Friday nights,
        my parents, brother & me at the table,
how my father would rip the hinge of the pizza box
        to make more room for drinks, the Parcheesi board.

From the height of that bridge, maples rippled
        their last flames, & when the guide called
for the vote, I told my husband I prefer the one
        he makes: thin as cardstock, mushrooms,

taleggio buttery as memory, rings
        of sautéed leeks. Yet I don't know
what I was expecting or why
        I should be surprised, but I hated the one

we ordered the night
        before my father died & that god-awful
silence of everyone pausing to look at him
        before we opened the box.

Italian Lessons at the Ear, Nose and Throat Doctor

We still carry them forward, somehow,
each language gesture a self-contained universe,
a wormhole into the lives of others as we are.

SANDRO BARROS

In the waiting room, I watch a child open
quadrants of sandpaper, running fingers
on it like Braille. On the TV, a squirrel
on its hind legs with its range of vocals,

head in the bowels of pumpkin, a bear in honey.
I open my phrasebook and think I could lick
this language off my fingers: the chug of the C, trill
of the R, the staccato I, the penultimate syllabication:

Mi piacerEbbe un biCCHIiere di vino. (I'd like a glass
of wine); *Il sole non si sente bene?* (Doesn't the sun
feel good?) What do people lose when they lose
a language? My grandparents stopped speaking

Italian to their children. I wonder if anyone heard
it in the river's frolic or in the deep rumble
of boiling water? Years later, translations
are a platter of stories and songs, out of reach

at the other end of the table. I want to describe
for you in Italian my father's recipe, passed
down from his parents, passed down
from their parents—the last shards of garden:

carrots, celery, onion, peppers, tomatoes,
preserved in vinegar, pressed in a pot with a rock
and canned. These gifts of glass. Or maybe it's enough
to say: *Per Favore. Ecco.* (Please. Here.)

The child in the waiting room now stands,
tests me: *Did you know the laughing
owl is extinct?* In a film, I thought I saw a hand
paint the letters *suffer* on a cave wall. No—

they were figures drowning. Sometimes I wake
panicked, feeling I might let go of a hand,
a faceless someone hanging off a cliff.
Then the dove's cry outside: *Don't, don't.*

Landscape with Woman, Cat, Eclipse

The cat she called a good cat was parading his ample
robe of fur, the broken sidewalk spooling carpet-like
to the horizon, silhouettes distorting to phantoms,
light shifting dim to dusk, herons climbing from
roosting places, lotus flowers closing. This scene
strange & silent: the cat calm knowing he is the object
of gaze, for when my neighbor muttered, *euthanizing soon,*
low in the sky, shadow appeared in the final seconds,
a deep gray. This cat contemplated his path as if
in Vipassana meditation, as if to say, *I become the grass,
the next cat, the subject of a poem by a poet walking past
who's thinking nothing dies.*

FROM CELLAR TO TABLE

Fennel

Arm of an ossified
angel found among
the root families. That perennial

note: you were on the wild
side, hard at the core, a verdant
taste with a venture

of licorice. Prometheus,
in his boldness and intelligence,
scaled a mountain and lifted

a stalk to light a flame
from the gods, which makes
me think remedy, which makes

me think raw: a mandoline
ski slope, the bright
flowers you bring, kiss

of oil and citrus, delicate fronds,
sometimes shaves
of parmesan, then a baked

frittata primavera followed by a slow-
roast chicken with shallots.
How they said you'd be good together,

how the braised becomes silky,
near melted.

My Happy Place

Subbituminous, dark as land or skin or death,
      strong when they were called dago
and wop, strong when the evenings crumbled:
      news of a miner killed by a fall of roof;

      a miner killed by a fall of slate at an entry; my
          great grandfather killed by a fall at the face
of a coal pillar; another child—my grandparents'
      baby, dead from diphtheria.
My ancestors pitched out a language
      like a broken tamboro.

They hid customs like snails they plucked
      off the basement wall who'd escaped
from the bucket—they quick-sucked them dry.
      My ancestors would rise, running

      bakeries out of garages, restaurants
          out of houses: pizza, hand-
dipped ricotta, hand-cut cavatelle, meats
          hanging from the cellar's old pipes.
They grew front yard gardens: lemon trees,
      chicories, peaches big as the fists

my grandparents shook when they woke
      to find their own garden ripped and ruined.
They never grew a garden like that again.
      What was it like to be forced to live

      in a new land? Was there struggle? Defeat?
          Exhilaration? I went to the homeland,
took a footpath by the sea. I wanted to walk alongside
          grapes clustering. I can tell you they tasted
like syrup, sun, wet stone; that before I took one
      from its trailing vine, it trembled.

Swordfish

You haunted me first in *The Perfect Storm*,
exhibitionist, frolic and joy turned
over the air before you were harpooned,
skin without scales grazed by an oiled sun.

What great leap to rid the self, no anchor,
no parasites, ectothermic, one blue
eye a wide fired bowl. I won't order
the catch of the day, impaled by toothpicks,

stuffed with capers off the Sicilian coast.
Still, the waiter bent like a rib of scythe,
leaned in close to describe your three-foot sword:
mercury, machine of bill, bone and breath;

how you stunned and slashed, though spearing was rare,
but once, a fisherman dove in the sea,
and after freeing his line that'd been caught,
turned to see you coming at high speed, frantic—

Turning Up *Moonstruck*

And I bake bread, bread, bread. And I sweat!
RONNY CAMMARERI (NICHOLAS CAGE)
Moonstruck, 1987

I've always gone for the younger
        brother, scruff & a wounded
demeanor, a modest kitchen, the glass
        of J&B. I want an undressed
pasta, the soundtrack of delivery trucks,
        a Brooklyn sidewalk, trees pearled
& snow falling like gnats swarming.
        They say a full moon
intensifies insomnia, transforms human
        into wolf. It can propel the risk
of disease. It might stave off debt;
        cause death. It can make you pass out;
trigger relatives to stop by unannounced.
        They say never mock a moon or lift
a finger to the moon & how one seen over
        the right shoulder brings good luck;
one over the left, bad. Let's bury superstitions
        rich as yolk, gather the gray
moths of worry, carefully wrap our losses
        growing quiet as the dough rises.
The bloody steak doesn't care what we'll do.
        The howling can't judge what it becomes.
So turn up *La bohème*, then lie down with me
        & throw those last loaves of loneliness
into the oven. After, love, we'll open one eye
        to the white sheet of night.

October

It's all about sturdy boots,
oversized suede gloves,

> how trees remove
> their leaves one by one,

how logs make their tent,
steadied in a fire, an evening

> flushed, transcendent,
> everything

falling to hollow
like opened wine, mouths, hands:

> time of fiber, maul,
> knot & branch,

this bend in the knees,
this arc in your spine.

Limoncello

I remember sky peeling
above the umbrella tree,
and Ravello's cloudy
eye inspecting the chill
of the Aspromontes.
Forgive me this poem
of one sweet note, but
after roasted branzino,
chard with oil, a tart
with mascarpone, good
God, the night glistens
like syrup, like homes
painted green-yellow-
green above the sea.
It's like lifting the base
of a gown, or you, love,
raising the crisp
sleeves of your shirt
on a passeggiata
through the liquid
light of a walled village.

Cypresses, after Visiting My Ancestral Village

That summer, I caught a ride on the back of a truck, passing
a fence of them, green as heaven's lifted blanket, fragrant
as regret,   each one   perfect   as a new story,   a concept
not unlike mourning, the sun dappling the cones,   leaves
stirring, all the little lights   there   then gone, each flicker
I think must have been someone who loved me,   someone
I might have loved.

Pasta Maker

I pour flour onto the laminate, form a well.
The yolks enchant, I think, like conjoined
suns or a lagoon of stewed apricots at the base
of Mt. Etna. I pull scrapings from the walls
into liquid. Here, nothing collapses, no fear,
though I am hopelessly rough and messy.
I knead, the satin elasticity alive in my hands.
You're at my side, all shiny and hoisting
the CucinaPro Imperia, reliable as steel.
I watch you carry the sfoglia like a freshly
ironed dress to a bed of semolina, lift our
pot on the stove. This time, I dot ricotta
down the sheet; you brush the perimeter
with water. You secure the top layer;
I press the mold, and after we gather
scraps into a ball, after all the time passed,
we savor cuscinetti— seven pillows each,
wading in truffle oil, melted butter, a leaf
of crispy sage. Oh, how we zest. Oh, how
we drink. Isn't this marriage, afterall? How
one feeds, the other gently cranks the handle,
supporting on the other side. *Great, one more,*
one of us will coach, and with anticipation
and surety we'll repeat, each notch to the next
setting until we've got the precise length and
fineness, light shining through— almost sheer.

Ode to Biscotti

An excuse for dessert
any time of day, my father

used to say. Winter mornings
my mother made eight kinds:

the classic cantuccini version
with almonds, anise extract,

or cocoa-macadamia, while
my father at the Formica table

explained how the non-perishable
food was valuable during journeys

and wars, a staple of the Roman
legions. Ah, to bake and bake twice,

to swim all the luxurious afternoon
sipping hazelnut or pistachio air

or a savory seeded sesame or asiago-
walnut especially satisfying with cheese.

It's March, and I'm dipping a leftover
fig and cinnamon in my coffee

over the sink, wishing my father
had held up through spring.

CORNERS AND MINIATURE

Robins Outside the Eat'n Park

Coffee with cream, two mugs, bacon
sputtering on a flat-top grill. You smiled
at everyone. I pierced a flower pad
of butter & you swallowed two pain

pills with juice. I learned you & Mom
come for the soup sometimes; how they
do a good fish sandwich, how the salad bar
is freshest on Saturday, how to clutch

towers of Styrofoam containers of pie
out over the icy lot, pack them in the car's
back seat. As we turned onto the road, we
spotted robins foraging—ten we counted

before they took flight. *They've usually left
by now*, you explained, but what you were
trying to say was that you'd die in two weeks.
If I could change anything, I wish I could have

stopped your tremors at the end, so violent
at times, I felt the valley's sixty-foot wall of rock
would crumple. Father, tell me what it's like
to climb darkness, cities reduced to fireflies,

to neon lights on Earth's marquee. I keep seeing you
exiting the diner, inching your walker, the scarf
I got you from Rome flapping like a caught bird.
Your cap is on, gray as the Monongahela River,

its steely wandering an indifferent god. Lately,
I'm in a red booth across packets of mixed berry jam.

Less Acid Than Orange

A tug from the small-vine
grapes, an avocado half,
resting in its skin, already
sliced into pale crescents.
The wrinkled flesh
of a date. At the Greenland
Market, people consider

a variety of produce: hands
extend in a choreographed
dance, offering one another
samples. At the coffee bin,
someone holds the lid while
the other scoops it in, floral
beans clapping raucous

in their bags. Like the edges
of countries, smiles break
so wide, the world speaks
of it: *peace, beauty*, dark mountain
of tresses spilling out. We were
given hearts meant to open
like the peels of clementines.

Cleithrophobia

It's not so bad if a few people
are there, you can smile, chat
about how the weather is better
than at home, how their day's
going, politely push the button
for their floor, but alone is worse,

& the stairwell closed in with doors
dimly lit for six floors is no better.
Can't know if you can come & go.
People head home for the day,
doors don't open, a call button
fails, or you imagine worse,

it's the weekend, & you're closed
in a mirrored box with a carpet
to fret oxygen, dwindling water,
a cable snap, then drop into a yoga
pose to pass the time better
until the bell dings and the doors

open, you get off, go on with your day,
but not until you've held the button
for someone else, & no one even knows.

Visiting the Tree of Life Synagogue, November, 2018

In Pittsburgh, I walk under a canopy
I once jogged with dogs. Now, Shady Avenue oaks
    weep on this sidewalk. White nationalist violence
is fueled by a white supremacist. I return to a town

    where I once ran book club for teachers:
I Never Saw Another Butterfly. Number the Stars,
    my saying: *So this will never happen again.* Now
squirrels in Squirrel Hill do their stop-start-stop. I used to

    buy bread at Five Points Bakery a block down, now
plastic-wrapped bouquets fan into a mountain. Students
    I once read poetry to at John Minadeo School sang
at this congregation. Now, children lay down their paper

    doves. I pass names of eleven souls: Richard, Rose,
brothers Cecil & David, Joyce, Jerry— customer at
    my brother's store, couple Bernice & Sylvan, Daniel,
Irving, Melvin. Breath falls, petals of flowers.

    I used to plan lessons with teachers
at Smallman Street Deli. Two weeks ago on Facebook,
    I saw one of those teachers standing on that street,
protesting he who would not denounce hate. I walk back

    to my car avoiding a leaf blower. Somebody
asks me for directions. I do not know. I walk behind
    my old neighbors. I think of teaching, gun laws,
November, hope.

Italian Lessons in Mysticism

An uncle asked: *Why were they so hysterical?*
        He recalled elder women
on his side of the family who would break

into spontaneous wailing over anything—
        death, of course, but other things:
an argument, a betrayal, a defeat.

Once, in the corner of a funeral parlor, a scene
        that haunts me still. A woman screamed,
tore at her clothes, dropped to her knees.

She had to be escorted out of the room.
        I want to go back to my uncle and say,
the state. Say *landowners.* Say *wife.*

In the 19th century, Southern Italian women
        responded to poverty, subordination,
their sexualization. Tarantella. Pizzica, ecstatic

dances with psychological collapse, ritualized
        weeping, chanting, medicinal healing.
Why were they hysterical? They learned

from their mothers, who learned
        from their mothers, that expression
was a weapon. This was not a way of life.
        This was the remnants of war.

Little Palermo

For the eleven Italian immigrant men
who were lynched following their
acquittal in New Orleans in 1891

Because their brows looked like caterpillars.
Because they assumed a dock was a wooden pier
used as a welcome place or moorage for boats.
Because they blew into the gut of a pig, stuffed

it with garlic and exotic greens. Because they charged
less than competitors, fifty cents for a lunch special
of sausage or stuffed pepper with a hard roll and choice
of drink. Because the mayor told everyone the docks

"had become attractive to Southern Italians and Sicilians,
the most idle, vicious, worthless people among us, filthy
in their homes, spreading disease, without religion, pride,
truth, or any quality that makes a good citizen."

Because the press cried *mafia*. Because the word *dock*
means to remove a part of an animal. Because
hundreds with "in-between" skin were rounded up.
Because *to be in the dock* means to be on trial.

Because they wore a gold chain with Saint Jude,
and before baking, made the sign of the cross.

Lygrophobia

the terrier's bark / asphalt
    breaks / a horn / a near-

miss crash / a siren / where's
    it coming from / the PA

system / coming down from
    each sound / blood rush /

veins like rivers to fingers / back up
    like the torture of anticipating

a balloon at the pinnacle of burst /
    though there's no parade / no

carnival / just the roar & spin
    of the exhaust above the range /

the blender's torque /
    two-horsepower motor

& aircraft-grade blades jarring the vortex /
    how it can be that even Bach's bright-

throated flute & violin dialogue
    is all agitate / long-held high notes

preparing for the ritornello
    as the phone rings / the news

you fear / a name someone
    only meant to whisper.

We Return to Where We Were Born

There are very few islands so small
that are so far from any land.

ROBERT PLATT

Heading home, we siblings became water,
reminiscing that trip to Bermuda,
bodysurfing the waves with our father.
Children, we knew nothing of the Buddha,
how we're constantly changing, never safe,
that *upādāna*, Sanskrit for clinging,
also means fuel. We'd always been afraid
of building fires: of overfeeding,
their size doubling, or being distracted.
But after we'd nursed our father at home,
we stacked a pine pyramid, struck a match.
Which wave is a father on the ocean?
We both cried out when a warm current came.
Our father was holy, aflame.

Elixir for My Father

> into nothing but
> cool light.
>
> PABLO NERUDA,
> *Ode to the Watermelon*

Because you asked for something sweet,
we dragged out the blender, pulled out a tall glass.
The weight of this, a heavy newborn in summer.
You once cut cubes for us, piled them in a green bowl.

We dragged out the blender, pulled out a tall glass.
Mom tapped the next syringe, Jeff adjusted your cap.
You once cut cubes for us, piled them in a green bowl.
We angled the straw, told you of an elixir from the islands.

Mom tapped the next syringe, Jeff adjusted your cap.
The white pill of sun flickered through the Redbud tree.
We angled the straw, told you of an elixir from the islands,
because you were dying.

The white pill of sun flickered through the Redbud tree,
the weight of this, a heavy newborn in summer.
Because you were dying.
Because you asked for something sweet.

Ars Poetica II

Though one cannot see,
one can see some.

NATIONAL GEOGRAPHIC

This frog, not half

the width of a coin,

in the rain-wet folds

of a rose. For a while,

I want to climb in.

I want to live here.

THE DIALECTIC
OF INSIDE/OUTSIDE

Ode to Turning Fifty As My Husband Paints a Winter Scene

Everything stripped to essence,   no leafed thatch
in which to hide.   Birdsong possibly, no
ego-ed story,   just a hawk's screeching flash.
Where else   to trudge in the middle   of poles
in a painting   of snow?   There go three deer
startling   across the field.   *Relinquish*
is my thought,   how even the evergreens
welcome   the thick   architecture of ice.

Ophiophobia

The girl once saw snakes
everywhere
as she tried to fall
asleep. As she dreamed.
If she cracked an eye,
they would undulate
through vents or wrap
around curtain rods,
then tumble like tires
or sturdy tape rolls
onto her floor,
which she translated to mean
death. Of course,
the snake could not help
being the snake,
even loves
being the snake,
its legless body
basking the sun by day,
by night, a satin ribbon
traversing the leaves.
As the girl grew,
she came to know
loss can happen
at once—
there, the cracking
of skin. What to do,
but touch it
like fine tissue, place
it in a small bag or box.
She thinks of that
gesture from the Kaballah,
where snakes' heads are raised

like proud pharaohs
or shepherd's hooks,
a tight ring of them
surrounds her,
but from the back,
their heads resemble
lilies. A woman now,
when she spots
a snake, quick tear
from the brush, resplendent,
she loves them. She rakes
leaves on the side of her house,
and is happy
to find the garter snake
who's out, surprised
to see her.

Visiting My Mother the First Time after My Father Died (Broken Sestina)

Petunias spill from her apartment patio, two urns
flank each corner, chairs she got for a good price,
one she refinished in butter yellow, the other robin-
egg blue. She works mornings from home, checking
if patients' pacemakers are working, her own heart
regulated with medication. Noon, it's rice cakes,

nut butter, blueberries, clipping coupons, The Price
Is Right on, dog on her lap, dog at our feet, checking
if there are sales. Afternoons, it's birdseed, the Carhartt
rack, the bank. Late day, we push marigolds in urns,
sweep the common grill area where she says *caked*,
but I was sure she said *ached*. She hates Red Robin,

so we go to Eat'n Park for cod and chocolate cake,
come home to watch a movie, talk about the price
of long-term caregiving. We unwrap foiled hearts.
I pass Dad's cane resting on the window sill. Check
if she took her pills. Someday, I'll get used to Dad's urn
on his dresser. Outside at the bird bath, that robin
again. Birds everywhere.

The Poet Becomes Enzyme, Salt and Water

> Women who spend nine or more hours
> a week caring for an ill spouse increase
> their risk of heart disease two-fold.
>
> S.L. LEE, *American Journal*
> *of Preventive Medicine*

Mother, I can't stop thinking under a different
sky, you might have worn a linen dress, a shift
that fell to the knee. You both could have
hiked Cinque Terre, waded in the Mediterranean,

toured Brittany to Bordeaux, poured a white
in Argentina the scent of jasmine and melon,
or caught the gentle slope of a giraffe as she
lowered her head in the Tugela to drink.

I wanted better for you both, but Dad's disease
was too much. While he was dying, your own heart
leaked like fountain water through my cupped
hands. Who knew his illness would be the acute

din of a manual clock for thirty years? This guilt
throbs in my chest. I wish I could circulate
the backflow of blood. Remnants of rock and dust
would collide otherwise. I'd be cells oxygenating

the map of your body, making you say yes
all those years ago to that other man you met
at that function, though I would have never
been born.

How to Haunt Humans (From *The Complete Animals' Guide to Spells, Possession and Paranormal Activity*)

Bald Eagle - Make yourself seen in the sky's light
  to provoke weeping at their wasted lives.

Cone Snail - When they raise your shell to their ear,
  make the rushing sound, *What have you killed?*

Dog - Use your unblinking stare to shame them
  into wearing T-shirts that say, "I pee in the shower
  and pick my nose when no one's looking."

Frog* - Show up at the pond sunning on a rock
  until they reconcile childhood guilt at small-animal
  stomping and bludgeoning.

Garter Snake - See **Frog**.

Ibex (Pyrenean)** - Taunt in dewy whispers the word *Celia*,
  last of your kind, her skull crushed near the French border
  in the rain.

Jellyfish - Pull select Republican senators from their
  beach houses and martinis into the Euxine abyssal plain
  at the bottom of the Black Sea.

Koala - Spit a retching essence of piss and eucalyptus
  at climate change deniers.

Laughing Owl** - Bring on an acute case of tinnitus with
  your high-pitched chuckle, coo, your whistle, chatter, mew.

Otter - Charm the smartest youth to seek careers
related to endangered species management and water
and land use.

Quagga** - No one remembers you, though you
were regarded as homely. Haunt them until they look
you up. Until they learn to love others, to love themselves.

Tiger - See *Bald Eagle.*

Ulysses Butterfly - Flutter their delicate lives with Greek
irony.

Vulture - You do you.

Yunnan Box Turtle** - Strike turtle soup eaters with a strain
of non-lethal, though long-lasting, gastrointestinal disease
presenting with back hives and a 30-day head rash.

Zebra - Gather in numbers, the sunset orange-pink behind
you on the Niger. See *Tiger.*

* Will especially affect male poets.
** Denotes extinction. Powers tripled.

After Hearing from Contacts Quarantined in Italy, You Warn Facebook Friends

In the darkest days of the Cold War,
US Navy officials reported hearing
whales, many miles away, their songs

a dialectic across the ocean, traveling
at a speed five times greater than in air.
You are a solitary mammal. You click

likes, type updates, message articles,
memes in your feed like joker
cards: a media hoax, the common flu,

a petri dish in Wuhan. Never was there
so much irony, ambient hum and grunt,
how whales are loudest on the planet,

but human blare is at the same decibel level
used by whales to communicate. What
is the sound of distance, this cacophony

of defiance, othering, fear, ignorance? A blue
whale has a heart the size of a VW Superbug
and an aorta big enough to swim in. What

can you say, but you tried? You could have
navigated were it not for the noise. You would have
yelled louder, but they wouldn't have heard you.

Home Altar in the Year of a Pandemic

Layer it anywhere: window sill, ledge, bench, buffet table. Prayer books, holy cards, rosaries, a medal with a patron saint, a ceramic Madonna, relics if you have any, cloths in liturgical colors, a vase of fresh, dried or artificial flowers, a flask of miraculous water, portraits of fish and dogs and cats and dead and living relatives, a candelabra, a favorite feather, stone or shell, one blessed palm, a deity statue, string lights, a copper gong, quartz and amethyst if you like, a hand-written recipe, a lace doily, a trailing plant in a basket. What have you lost? Who among us does not need a comfort, magic? Bring on the cocoon, pile on the kitsch and avalanche, you merciless, bountiful harvest, let us drown in your song.

The Poet Asks, What Prevents You from Loving Yourself?

I don't have the patience to read a manual. I'm sad
my password is no longer my deadest dog. When my

mother asked if she could warm me soup, I said, *I can
take care of myself.* I can't stop thinking about the child

on a Florida beach who bludgeoned a live crab with a stick,
the parent did nothing. Palms in wind sound like rain. I miss

the important thing my love said. I hide in a house of books.
My father died because his nerves ate away at his own skin.

People tell me I'm calm, but I'm only trying to quiet
the heartbeat. My car stalls at night, and I panic. So many

headlines are some version of "Because Citizens Wanted
a Draining System to Remove Runoff in Low-Lying Swamp."

The sky is a gray awning. I mean to fill this space with forest
and animals. I wish I never learned to eat flesh. I can pinch

the dead off my plants with a thumbnail. In the year of three
deaths, it was the dog that made me collapse. I don't know

the name of the bird who sings, and never look it up. It might
be true what they say about Italian American women. I eat

joy like tangles of chicory. A man once told me what a shame
to have no babies with a baby-bearing body. My mother is

becoming a small bird I crouch to hug. I climb hills for elegy,
from my mouth, pull primrose.

Diagram of the Four Chambers of the Heart

half-hearted, missed beat
construction paper hearts
schoolkids who can't spell *crux* & *core*
chalky *Be Mine, Miss You* hearts
emojis with bows, emojis with arrows
hearts of families
doing the best they can like the rose

chocolates on the console. Happy, young
conservatives with border hearts
on their flyers, single-chambered sacs of
crustaceans screaming to the top of a kettle
heart of a pandemic, a protest. Thrashing
hearts of crows and elephants
next to one of their dead. Heart of us all

above the dead. Panic heart, strong heart,
be wide as a three-and-a-half-inch vise
a kind of god, soft & wise
recall the therapist who said, *Try to
stay in the moment.* Heart of a poet like balled paper
that big, round Buddha, mind clear liquid as
looking out the window, moved by the

how though diseased, can still
support the tree, & how the rabbit is
bounding the lawn, & when sadness comes, you
think of last night, roasted peppers, celery ribs, your love
peeled labels from Two Hearted IPAs, how you like
that first pierce of fried artichoke, a break from this
world, all this going on.

The Fact of a Room

When the last sun traces the pines, and shadows advance
like spirits, our procession upstairs is royalty. Overhead
lights dim to stars in reverence to our geometry of fitting.
Years, we've sipped evenings of mineral skin,
glasses of Greco di Tufo like that hour before supper
on a beach in Italy, shellfish quivering before a backdrop
of sea. Love, let's make the curtains billow and sigh. I want
to end with a sleep remembering open floor-length shutters,
a view of homes in arresting colors. I want this palest sky
painted around us on a bed of clouds.

Ode to My Mother-In-Law's Sunday Sauce

What kind do you want? she asks,
holding up bags like a butcher lifting
cuts of meat. Prosciutto-wrapped

dates and brined olives glisten
like jewels on the counter
near stools where we park.

Like children, we take turns.
My husband is spaghetti. I, rigatoni.
We've driven low hills of three

neighborhoods, wine padded
in a bag, a screwdriver sticking
out the front pocket. Outside,

her golden retriever and our Labrador
chase and tumble bare-teethed
under a blue heron rising.

Her sauce isn't as sweet as my
father's, but I prefer it that way, her
radio set to Andy Williams and his river.

My husband chops romaine, spinach,
cucumber, shallots. Our ritual
at a white-clothed table with a mason jar

of hydrangea from her garden.
My mother in-law teaches me
how fresh pepper awakens everything,

how to be alone and fill the hours
with making art, reading mysteries,
watering ivy, combing a dog's hair.

One of fifteen children, she teaches me
how to lose an eleventh sister,
if I'd had any sisters.

What is it about this elixir
that entwines history, talk, memory?
The chemistry

of tomato interacts with basil,
bay leaf, onion, a narrative evolving,
yielding something new,

something we can keep
in the fridge for days. Tonight,
I will sleep, I think, as I clear

dishes, sip the last of my wine,
squeeze Dawn© for her
in a silver pot in this sage cottage

full of the faces she's painted:
a woman pouring milk, lilies
under a bridge, a Realist portrait

of a family, a man reclined in a chair,
his expression turned to the fire,
Jules Breton's *Song of the Lark*,

and a peasant girl grasping earth,
looking toward home.

My dog is depressed,

he sits taxidermied in a patch of grass, an island
far from our lounges, his bag of treats, our Sun
Chips. It is April, and he'd normally be here

beside us or wedging his nose in mole holes
or the neighbor's corner fence. Or suddenly lifting
his muzzle like a German chef who was trained

in France, catching nuances of the bone he stashed
last week, fresh-cut grass, bloodroot, or a soupçon
of mushrooms from the river bottom.

The dog in the adjacent backyard to ours is gone—
not dead gone, but moved gone,
but Maddox doesn't know that, this dog

for seven years he bolted to, barked at, sniffed,
a dog he never saw but through a crack
in the fence, which was everything.

Dusk, he still rouses under hunter orange skies,
thinking he smelled a rustling and begins that Weimaraner
tiptoe to the fence. While nighttime, he sits

trembling by our darkened patio table for hours.
My dog knows this world of loss, pays attention
to the slivers of time between my blinks,

knows about rain, that there's no grace
in leaving without saying anything.
I saw our neighbor's Flat-Coated Retriever

that morning of their departure from the passenger
side of a U-Haul pulling away down Grand River Avenue, chin
weaving out a partially-opened window.

He was looking, too, lips in a gummy, toothy grin,
nosing the most wondrous wind.

NOTES

The second opening epigraph is from W. S. Merwin's poem "The Wine" published in the spring, 1973 issue of *The Hudson Review*.

The third opening epigraph is from Gaston Bachelard's book *The Poetics of Space* (London, England: Penguin Classics, 1958/1964).

"Agoraphobia": The epigraph for this poem is from Jennifer Militello's collection *Body Thesaurus* (North Adams, MA: Tupelo Press, 2013).

"My Happy Place": In stanzas one and two, the lines "killed by a fall of slate at an entry" and "killed by a fall at the face/ of a coal pillar" are from the Coal Miners Memorial Millwood Shaft Mine document from the Joseph D'Andrea Papers, Detre Library Archives, Pittsburgh, PA.

"Limoncello": The word *passeggiata* means "evening stroll."

"Approaching the Tree of Life Synagogue: November, 2018" is in memory of the eleven souls massacred in the October 27, 2018 mass shooting in Pittsburgh, PA.

"Little Palermo": Though minor in comparison to Black suffering, the story in this poem is indebted to an article in *Italian Americana*, "Protection of Italian Laborer on U.S. Soil: Proposals of a Federal Anti-Lynching Law and Relations Between Italy and the United States" by Patrizia Fama Stahle, Winter, 2017.

"We Return to Where We Were Born": The epigraph for this poem is from Robert Platt's article "The Significance of the Location of Bermuda" in *The Journal of Geography*, 1921.

"Elixir for My Father": The epigraph for this poem is from Pablo Neruda's collection *All the Odes* (New York, NY: Farrar, Straus and Giroux, 2017).

"After Hearing from Contacts Quarantined in Italy, You Warn Facebook Friends": The lines describing the whale's heart size are adapted from my friend, Karenanna Boyle Creps.

"My dog is depressed": Some language in this poem is adapted from Temple Grandin's book *Animals Make Us Human* (Boston, MA: Houghton Mifflin Harcourt, 2009).

ACKNOWLEDGMENTS

I will always be grateful to Corey Van Landingham for selecting ELIXIR, and to David Bowen and the team at New American Press. I'm equally grateful to Maria Terrone for selecting ELIXIR, and I thank Nicholas Grosso, Fred Gardaphé, Anthony Tamburri, and everyone at Bordighera Press. Thanks to my teachers, especially Dan Albergotti for his generosity and insight, Laura Apol, Billy Collins, Sarah Freligh, TR Hummer, Major Jackson, Diane Kendig, Matthew Olzmann and Marge Piercy. My appreciation to my department chair, Dorinda Carter Andrews, and dean, Robert Floden, for supporting work in the arts; and Doug Gage, Jeff Cole and Sue Sipkovsky for their expertise with an MSU humanities and arts grant to begin writing the poems. I thank Melissa Marinaro from Pittsburgh's Heinz History Center for her assistance with navigating the Detre Library and Archives. Dear friend, Robin Silbergleid, gave sage feedback on the manuscript, and others offered critical eyes and kind hearts, especially Sherine Gilmour, Chuck Madansky, James Wyshynski, the Cherry Point poets (Michelle Ott, Don Cellini, Diane Henningfeld, Jonie McIntire and Beth Myers), Alecia Beymer, Karenanna Boyle Creps, Wendy DeGroat, Telaina Eriksen, Marianne Peel Forman, Stephanie Glazier, Scott Jarvie, Cori McKenzie, Cindy Hunter Morgan and Wilderness Sarchild. I thank my colleagues, students, friends and family for their support. The writing of ELIXIR was buoyed by the love and support from my mother, Connie Puntureri, my brother, Jeff, and my dog, Maddox, often at my feet as I wrote. And my father, Carl Puntureri, who I know would have been so proud. Most of all, I thank my husband, Steve, for being my first reader and editor, for his encouragement, love and listening, for being the best kind of elixir.

Grateful acknowledgment is also made to the editors of the following journals in which these poems have appeared, sometimes in slightly different versions or with different titles:

About Place Journal: "Visiting the Tree of Life Synagogue, November, 2018"

Crab Creek Review: "Elixir for My Father;" "Sibling with Hair on Fire. Sibling Tangled in Vines."

Cream City Review: "Agoraphobia"

Emrys Journal: "One Life Burning"

FWJ Plus: "Childhood Friends"

Gastronomica: "Limoncello"

The Greensboro Review: "Lygrophobia"

The Ilanot Review: "Fennel"

Italian Americana: "The Fact of a Room;" "Turning Up Moonstruck"

The Main Street Rag: "My Father Asks What I Think Happens after We Die;" "Robins Outside the Eat'n Park;" "Cypresses, After Visiting My Ancestral Village"

Mid-American Review: "Holding Hands on the Bank. Leaves Float down the River"

The National Poetry Review: "After Rescuing the Dying Butterfly from My Sidewalk"

New Ohio Review: "Drag Heavy Pot to Shed"

Nimrod International Journal: "Diagram of the Four Chambers of the Heart;" "Dear Australia;" "Ode to Pizza;" "The Poet Asks, What Prevents You from Loving Yourself?;" "My Dog is Depressed;" "After Hearing from Contacts Quarantined in Italy, You Warn Facebook Friends;" "Home Altar in the Year of a Pandemic"

Ofi Press: "When They Named the Egret and Kept Feeding Her"

Ovunque Siamo: "Italian Lessons at the Ear, Nose and Throat Doctor;" "Ode to Biscotti;" "Ode to My Mother-in-Law's Sunday Sauce"

Pittsburgh Poetry Journal: "The Childfree Couple"

Pittsburgh Post-Gazette: "Halftime"

Pittsburgh Quarterly: "Highland Meadows, Allegheny County, 1979"

Quiddity: "We Return to Where We Were Born"

River Heron Review: "Losing a Religion"

Split Rock Review: "How to Haunt Humans: From *The Complete Animals' Guide to Spells, Possession and Paranormal Activity*"

Third Wednesday: "Landscape with River, Man, Mountain"

Vox Poetica: "Less Acid Than Orange"

Drag Heavy Pot to Shed and *Holding Hands on the Bank. Leaves Float down the River* were reprinted in the REO Town Reading Anthology edited by Matthew Rossi (Michigan State University's Cube Program, 2020)

Drag Heavy Pot to Shed was a finalist for the 2018 New Ohio Review Poetry Prize

Agoraphobia was a finalist for the 2019 Cream City Review Summer Prize in Poetry and in the 2019 Sewanee Review Poetry Contest

Landscape with River, Man, Mountain was named Honorable Mention for the 2016 Third Wednesday Poetry Prize and the 2016 Connecticut River Review Poetry Prize

Dear Australia; Ode to Pizza; The Poet Asks, What Prevents You from Loving Yourself?; My Dog is Depressed; After Hearing from Contacts Quarantined in Italy, You Warn Facebook Friends; Home Altar in the Year of a Pandemic received second prize in the 2020 Pablo Neruda Poetry Prize

Losing a Religion was a finalist for the 2019 River Heron Review 2019 Poetry Prize and the 2019 Indiana Review Poetry Prize

Elixir for My Father was a semi-finalist for the 2019 Crab Creek Review Poetry Prize

Diagram of the Four Chambers of the Heart was a semi-finalist for the 2019 Pablo Neruda Poetry Prize

ABOUT THE AUTHOR

JANINE PUNTURERI CERTO is also author of the full-length poetry collection *IN THE CORNER OF THE LIVING* (Main Street Rag, 2017). Her poems appear or are forthcoming in *The Cincinnati Review*, *The Greensboro Review*, *Italian Americana*, *Mid-American Review*, *New Ohio Review*, *Poetry Northwest*, *Shenandoah*, *Vallum* and others. Her poems earned second prize in *Nimrod*'s 2020 Pablo Neruda Prize for Poetry. Born in Pittsburgh with degrees from the University of Virginia (MA) and Virginia Commonwealth University (Ph.D), she lives in East Lansing, Michigan where she is an associate professor at Michigan State University.

NEW AMERICAN POETRY PRIZE

Since 2010, New American Press has awarded an annual prize to recognize emerging writers of compelling and innovative poetry in all forms and styles.

JANINE CERTO. *Elixir*. 2020.
EMILY MOHN-SLATE. *The Falls*. 2019.
SARAH ARONSON. *And Other Bodiless Powers*. 2018.
KIT FRICK. *A Small Rising Up in the Lungs*. 2017.
CHRISTOPHER COKINOS. *The Underneath*. 2016.
BRITTNEY SCOTT. *The Derelict Daughter*. 2015.
ARNE WEINGART. *Levitation for Agnostics*. 2014.
DAMIEN SHUCK. *The Drowning Room*. 2013.

2012 contest renamed "2013" to reflect the year when prize was awarded.

PAUL NEMSER. *Taurus*. 2011.
STEPHEN HAVEN. *The Last Sacred Place in North America*. 2010.

LAURIA/FRASCA POETRY PRIZE

The prize was conceived to promote the poetry of the Italian diaspora in English. Quality poetry in any style and on any theme is sought.

MATTHEW CARIELLO. *Talk*. Vol. 1. 2018
JANET SYLVESTER. *And Not to Break*. Vol. 2. 2019
JANINE CERTO. *Elixir*. Vol. 3. 2020

CPSIA information can be obtained
at www.ICGtesting.com
Printed in the USA
LVHW021108121021
700211LV00006B/785